Christmas Ornaments

CAROLYN VOSBURG HALL

Published by

Krause Publications
700 E. State St.
Iola, WI 54990-0001

Please call or write for our free catalog of publications. Our toll-free number to place an order or obtain a free catalog is 800-258-0929, or please use our regular business telephone 715-445-2214.

02-03 QB9.71

Photography by Carolyn Vosburg Hall, unless otherwise noted.

Illustrations by Carolyn Vosburg Hall.

Project designs by Carolyn Vosburg Hall, unless otherwise noted.

ISBN: 0-87349-442-3

02-03

Acknowledgments:

Thanks to my editor Jodi Rintelman, book designer Marilyn Hochstatter, cover designer Kim Schierl, and all the staff at Krause Publications for creative support.

This book is dedicated
to my brother, Bob,
who took me Christmas
shopping as a child.
Imagine our mom's
surprise when we spent
our Christmas gift
allowance on
ornaments.

Contents

Introduction

When you open that box of Christmas tree ornaments, memories of all the delights of the season come popping out. All of your decorations, especially the handmade ones, can embody warm personal messages. Who doesn't have a collection of special ones—your child's handprint in plaster, a glued macaroni star, or an elegant hand-sewn Santa? Making your own ornaments gives you the pleasure of creation, lasting decorations for your tree, and treasured gifts for friends.

All ages, from kids to grandmas, will find pleasure in making their own ornaments. Children like to use easy, quick materials and techniques to make ornaments. Artists use their more technical skills to make them from blown, fused, or stained glass; engraved gold or silver metals; modeled and fired clay; or carved wood. The skill level required for most projects in this book fits in between. They focus on readily available materials and show doable techniques. Some take a half hour to make while others, like the Japanese Temari ball, could takes hours and hours. Not to worry, this gives you more time to contemplate how pleased the recipient of your gift ornament will be.

Handmade ornaments are a delight to make, a joy to give, and a pleasure to hang on your Christmas tree.

Christmas is celebrated in many lands and many ways. Knowing some of this lore makes the theme of each Christmas ornament more interesting. Some of these traditions are ancient ones that include such icons as evergreen trees, wreaths, mistletoe, candles, bells, and holly. Some feature religious symbols such as crèches, angels, and guiding stars. Others show more recent themes such as Santas, stockings, toys, gingerbread houses, and elves. No ornament shape is more enduring than colorful balls in many styles, and none symbolizes Christmas more than a star on top of the tree.

Along with these bits of traditional lore, you'll find full-color photos of each ornament, lists of materials, patterns, illustrations, and instructions to make them. So collect your box of supplies—beads, ribbons, fabrics, chenille stems, sequins, and shiny papers—and let's begin.

This small cone-shaped tree is made from pinecones that were gathered outside and spray-painted a festive metallic gold. Designed by Phyllis Zacherle.

Tips for making ornaments

Ornaments, by their nature, are fragile. At our house, a few of those exquisite glass balls explode on the hard floor every year. The fragile ones are like flowers, meant to bloom a short while and then fade. Yet when packed away with care, even fragile ornaments, including your hand-made treasures, can last for years and years.

Choose lightweight, yet sturdy materials to construct your ornaments. Heavy ornaments will cause tree limbs to sag. Ornaments that are too fragile won't survive until next season. Certain materials are suggested in the instructions for best results, but others may do. For example, the folded Christmas tree can be made from a variety of papers, thin sheets of plastic, or even stiff fabric.

Store your ornaments in sturdy boxes. If you can find them, use special boxes with dividers. Wrap the fragile ornaments in tissue paper and pack them in these separate compartments. Over the summer, make sure your ornaments are stored away from extreme heat or dampness.

You can leave the lights and ornaments on an artificial tree, if you have a place to store it. If so, be sure to bend the hooks closed, both on the ornaments and the limbs, and wrap the tree in a large plastic bag to store (available for live tree disposal). Move the tree back in place next year, and add some new touch, such as a wire-edged ribbon or special new ornaments. New ideas hit the store shelves every holiday season.

Select the right kinds of glue and paint for the materials you're working with (product labels will list this information). For example, some beads will require hot jewelry glue, and Shrinky Dinks® plastic needs waterproof paint or pencils. For your ornament making session, collect ornament materials from everywhere—candy ribbons, costume jewelry, art papers, and on craft store safaris.

Include family and friends in making these small decorative projects. Part of the joy of Christmas is being with people you love. Another part is giving gifts; and the ornaments you make will be fine gifts.

We wish you a
Merry Christmas.

Left. Sparkling crystal ornaments collected over many years by Phyllis Zacherle glitter on this theme Christmas tree.

Right. Flick on the tiny colored lights, and the clear crystal ornaments turn red.

1 Candles and Holly Clip

Traditional candles for the tree are safer made from a glue stick (for a hot glue gun), ribbons, shiny paper, and a hair clip.

The song *Deck the Halls with Boughs of Holly* brings to mind waxy green holly leaves and carolers with lighted candles, singing joyful songs. From early times, people have used evergreens and lighted candles to celebrate the winter solstice. These items symbolize renewed life and celebrate the beginning of longer days.

As time passed, ancient rites combined with Christian celebrations in many countries for the biggest event of the year. On St. Lucia Day (December 13) in Sweden, the oldest daughter dresses in white and wears an evergreen wreath with seven lighted candles on her head to serve family members coffee and buns in bed. The Jewish Festival of Lights features a candelabrum for nine candles. In Germany, people put lighted candles on their evergreen trees and in their windows as a sign of welcome. Now Christmas is a wonderful hodge-podge of traditions collected from many lands.

YOU NEED

- 3" x ½" glue stick, wooden dowel, or candle
- 1½" x 18" metallic or dark green wrapping paper
- 1½" hair clip
- 1" x ¼" metallic gold ribbon
- 24" x 1¼" red and gold metallic ribbon*
- 3 red berries with wire stem
- 4" florist wire
- Glue gun, awl or sharp tool, scissors

Used in this project: ribbon saved from a Godiva® chocolate box.

1. For the candle, drill or poke a small hole in the top of the glue stick. For the flame, clip one end of the gold ribbon at an angle. Twist the other end to a point. Dab the pointed end with glue and force it into the hole.

2. Cut off the bottom of the glue stick at an angle to fit one side of the hair clip. Firmly glue the glue stick onto the clip handle, but avoid interfering with the spring action.

3. Cut five or six holly leaves from the green paper, and punch a hole in the base of each.

4. Form the red and gold ribbon into a bow, and twist the wire around the center of the bow and the holly berry stems. Thread the wire through the holly leaves and around the center of the bow.

5. Wire the bow onto the clip handle at the base of the glue stick. Arrange the leaves and glue them in place.

LEAF PATTERN

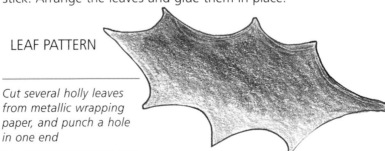

Cut several holly leaves from metallic wrapping paper, and punch a hole in one end

"*K*iss me," says the mistletoe ball. The old British custom of hanging the ball in doorways means anyone may steal a kiss from the person standing under it.

Mistletoe, considered sacred for thousands of years, was said to cause enemies meeting under it to throw down their weapons and embrace. Further, it was said that sprigs of mistletoe hung over the baby's crib prevented theft by fairies and promoted dreams of immortality. Mistletoe hung in the home signified purity, strength, happiness, peace, and romance.

This plant also has medicinal value, but it is poisonous. The traditional shape of the ball comes from boughs bent into circles.

Mistletoe, possessor of magical qualities, invites people to kiss under the cluster of leaves and berries.

1. For leaf veins, clip 10 wires 4" long. Glue a wire to each of 10 large wooden ovals, centered lengthwise with one end protruding.

2. Mix the paints to make a warm green color, and paint both sides of all 17 leaves and wire stems.

3. Wire the leaf stems into a cluster. Glue the small oval leaves into the cluster.

4. Loop the remaining wire six times into a 5" circle, or use a 5" wooden embroidery hoop. Twist the leaf stems onto the circle at the joint.

5. Twist the wire-edged ribbon loosely around the circle to cover the wire or hoop. Form a ribbon bow at the top. Tie the narrow ribbon around the center of the wide bow to secure it to the circle. Tie the narrow ribbon in a bow.

6. Glue the pearl beads at the cluster of stems for berries.

YOU NEED

- 8 feet of wire
- Ten 2" wooden ovals and seven 1¼" wooden ovals*
- 36" red and green 1½" wire-edged ribbon
- 15" x ¼" gold ribbon
- 6mm pearl beads*
- Green acrylic paint (mix white, green, gold)
- Glue gun, pliers with cutter, paintbrush, scissors

Used in this project: Forster Woodsies® assorted wooden pieces, Darice® Craft Designer beads.

Thin wooden disks, pearl beads, ribbon, and wire assemble into a mistletoe ball.

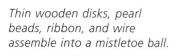

3 Embossed Bell

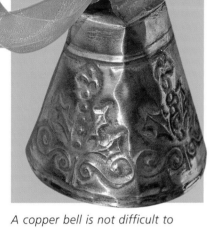

"Sleigh bells ring, are you listening?" goes the first line of the song *Walking in a Winter Wonderland*. Even better known is the Christmas carol *Jingle Bells*. The Christmas season means not only beautiful sights, entrancing smells, and exciting textures, but also the wonderful sounds of bells and carols heralding the event. From tiny tinkling bells to clanging carillon bells, the bells ring out their joyous sounds. In Norway during the festival called "ringe in Julen" (ringing in Christmas), people ring church bells at 5:00 p.m. on Christmas Eve. Another sound to open our hearts is the ringing of bells by Salvation Army volunteers for charity. And nothing is more romantic than sleigh bells on the horse's harness as you glide over the glistening snow.

A copper bell is not difficult to make, if you have a thin sheet of copper and a stylus to engrave the designs.

You Need

- 5" x 7" sheet of medium-weight copper
- 24" x ¾" sheer amber-colored ribbon
- 16" x ⅛" metallic gold ribbon
- 10 metallic gold ⅜" bead rings
- Brown or green acrylic paint
- 2" diameter tube or rod to shape the ball
- Stylus (or skewer, knitting needle, or pencil), scissors, padded surface, nail, pliers, glue gun

Used in this project: ArtEmboss® malleable metal sheets for crafts.

Copper ornaments, the handmade bell or the store-bought acorn, enhance Christmas wrappings.

1. Lay the copper on the padded surface, and place the pattern over it. Use the stylus or skewer to trace (and emboss) the design lines.

2. Traced lines will puff up on the reverse side. For extra puff, retrace the lines from the reverse side. To delineate the lines, outline them on the front with the stylus. Add texture to the background by embossing the copper with dots, circles, or linear patterns if desired.

3. For a faux patina, brush brown or green acrylic paint into the front. Buff the color off the surface with a cloth or sponge, leaving color in the crevices.

4. Cut out the bell with scissors and punch a hole in the top with the nail. Clip along the lower edge. Use pliers to turn under an ⅛" rim along the curved edge. Press flat.

5. Gently shape the bell over a tube to round it. The designs will not shape as easily as the blank spaces. Hot glue the side flap to the bell edge. Fold the short flaps inward. Fold the long flaps inward and upward. Align the holes, apply glue, and press the two top flaps together. Thread the gold ribbon through the holes, and tie it in a bow.

6. For the hanging cord, thread the ⅛" ribbon evenly through the hole. Loop the two ends back and forth through the bead rings, and tie a loop at the top.

The engraved design stiffens the copper sheet, resulting in an antique-looking bell.

Cut 1

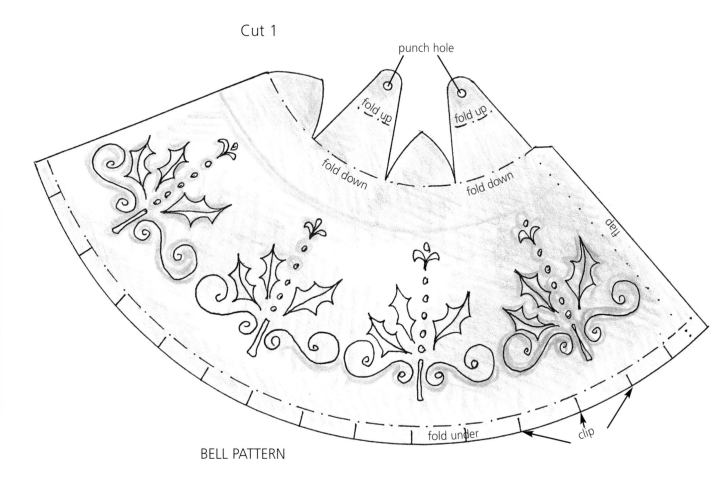

BELL PATTERN

4 Santa Claus Coat

"Ho, ho, ho," means Santa Claus is coming to town. Santa, the symbol of Christmas giving, has many names—Saint Nicholas in Europe; Santa Claus in the United States, Canada, and Australia; Father Christmas in the United Kingdom and Ireland; Pere Noel in France; and Weihnachtsman in Germany. Children grow up to recognize Santa as a myth, yet his spirit still perpetuates the reality of a generous spirit. Now dads, charity volunteers, or department store employees may dress as Santa to celebrate gift giving. Some may worry that giving gifts strays from the spirit of Christmas as a religious occasion, but gift giving is among the oldest and best of human traditions.

This tiny Santa coat is made from a fashionable red lamé fabric with sequins printed on. It's lined in gold satin with faux fur trim along the hem.

YOU NEED

- 8" x 10" decorative red fabric (non-fraying for narrow seam allowances)
- 8" x 10" metallic gold fabric (for lining and buckle)
- 8" x 1" strip of ½" pile white faux fur fabric
- 5" x ¼" strip black felt
- 6" wire
- Sewing machine, scissors, glue, pliers

1. Photocopy or trace the coat pattern. Pin it to the folded red fabric, matching the pattern edge with the fabric fold, and cut it out. Repeat for the lining. Cut the buckle from gold felt and the belt from black felt.

2. Align the red and gold fabrics face-to-face and sew a seam from the coat front bottom (A) up around the neck to the other bottom edge (B). Sew the sleeve ends (C).

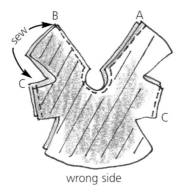

wrong side

turn right side

3. Turn right side out. Finger press the seam open.

4. Fold the red fronts facing the red back, aligning the underarm seams lining side out. Sew each side seam, back-stitching at the sleeve ends. Turn.

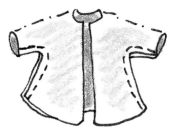

5. Align the fur face-to-face to the coat bottom edge, and sew along the raw edges. Open the seam, fold the fur over this seam, and hand stitch to finish.

6. Sew or glue the belt around the coat. Glue on the buckle.

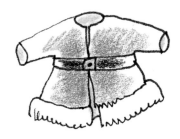

7. Bend the wire into the shape of a hanger, and put it into the coat.

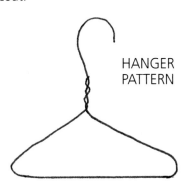

HANGER PATTERN

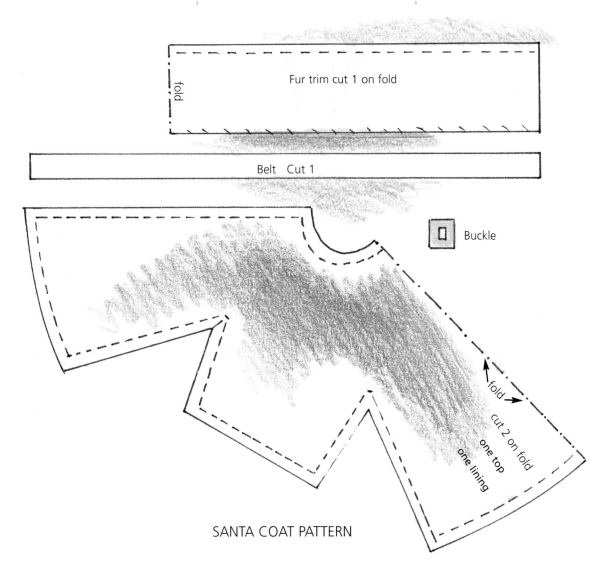

fold

Fur trim cut 1 on fold

Belt   Cut 1

Buckle

fold

cut 2 on fold
one top
one lining

SANTA COAT PATTERN

5 Elf Shoes

Santa Claus, as shown in *The Night Before Christmas* poem drawn by Thomas Nast, was a jolly old elf with a big round belly, red nose, and white beard. He wore a red suit trimmed in white fur with black boots. A more recent version shows a bearded Santa in a long flowing robe trimmed in fur, as Saint Nicholas might have dressed in medieval times.

In Germany, Knecht Rupert, the elf who is Saint Nicholas' assistant, gives presents to good children and whipping rods to bad ones (better be good!). An elf called Jultomten (Sweden) or Julenissen (Denmark and Norway) leaves presents for children. And everyone knows elves toil year round at the North Pole making Santa's toys. Elf shoes carry reminders of past eras when people really believed in tiny folk.

The brocade elf shoe is lined in metallic gold fabric, while the multicolored felt shoe is unlined, but both have an inner sole for stiffening.

YOU NEED

For both shoes
- ½" bead for toe
- 10" gold ribbon for hanging
- 1" fiberfill wad
- Sewing machine, scissors, paper, pencil, blunt skewer, pins, needle, and thread

For the felt shoe
- 2½" x 5" bright pink felt for upper
- 2½" x 5" lavender felt for upper
- 2" x 5" turquoise felt for sole

For the lined fabric shoe
- 3" x 10" blue/gold brocade for uppers
- 3" x 10" metallic gold fabric for the linings
- 2" x 5" purple felt for the sole
- 2" x 5" purple felt for the inner sole

TO MAKE THE FELT SHOE

1. Trace or photocopy the pattern, minus the seam allowance. Trace or pin the pattern to the felt, and cut two uppers, one sole, and an insole for stiffening.

2. Match the uppers, and sew the heel (A) to (B) and from (C) to the angle on the toe front (D).

3. Align the upper to the sole, matching (A) to (A) and (D) to (D). Begin at (D) and sew all around the sole to join. Leave overcast seams exposed, or turn the shoe. Add an insole and stuffing in the toe. Tuck in the inner sole to stiffen the sole.

The elf shoe can be cut from colors of felt and hand-sewn with exposed seams.

Tip Felt shoes can be hand stitched with the seams exposed. Fabric shoes will need a lining. On the lined shoe, the inside seams are covered with an insole.

1. Trace or photocopy the pattern, including the seam allowance (full pattern). Fold the fabric face-to-face (to reverse one side), and cut it out. Repeat for the lining.

2. Match the fabric and lining top edges, and sew across the top edge (center of photo). Clip the seam allowances on the inside curves and corners. Turn right sides out (bottom of photo).

3. Align the fabric uppers together and the fabric linings together. Pin at the seams (B) and (C). Sew from the fabric heel (A) to the lining heel (A). Match the toe seams (C) to (D) and sew from (D) to (B). The

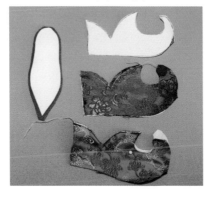

torn paper (top) helped stabilize the fabric while it slid through the sewing machine.

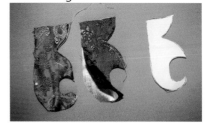

4. Use a blunt skewer to turn the toe and push in fiberfill. Tuck in the inner sole to cover the seams. Sew a bead or bell on the toe. Sew a ribbon or cord at the heel.

ELF SHOE PATTERN

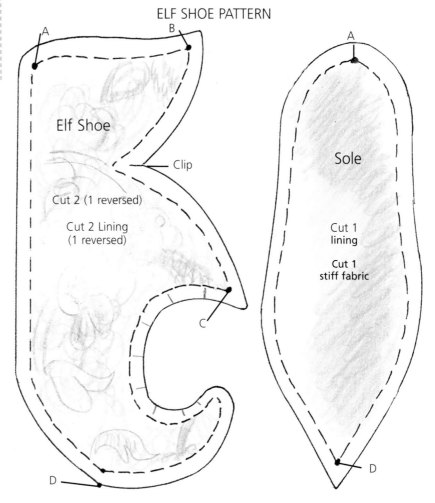

Elf Shoe

Clip

Cut 2 (1 reversed)

Cut 2 Lining
(1 reversed)

A   B   C   D

Sole

Cut 1
lining

Cut 1
stiff fabric

For the lined shoe, use the full pattern to cut out the pieces. For the felt shoe, use the pattern minus the seam allowances. You can trace or photocopy the pattern.

6 Christmas Stocking

For many of us, Santa Claus symbolizes gift-giving, yet the giving of gifts in the winter season dates back at least as far as ancient Rome and as wide as countries from Sweden to Japan. The most famous traditional gifts of Christmas are frankincense, gold, and myrrh brought by the Magi to the newborn Jesus.

For stocking gifts, the story goes that Saint Nicholas (called the Boy Bishop) knew three young women with no marriage dowry. To remedy this, he threw bags of coins down their chimney, which fell into their stockings. Thus the custom began for children to hang up their stockings near the fireplace for Santa to fill with treats. Fifty years ago they might have found a beautiful orange, a rare treat in winter in cold climates. Nowadays, candy and small gifts make mysterious lumps in the stockings on Christmas morn. Rumor went that bad children found lumps of coal from the Christmas witch.

In some countries, children put out their shoes for gifts and a plate full of cookies for Santa Claus.

This miniature 6-inch Christmas stocking ornament can still hold a tiny gift or two. Or you can double every pattern dimension to make a larger stocking.

YOU NEED

- 10" x 13" festive fabric (gold print shown)
- 16" x 2½" purple metallic fabric strip
- 7" x 1¼" copper metallic fabric
- 7" x 1¼" red/gold ribbon
- 8" x ¾" gold lacy ribbon
- 24" x ¾" green/gold ribbon
- 5 brass ⅜" bells
- Wad of stuffing
- Sewing machine, scissors

1. Trace or photocopy the pattern. Fold the fabric face-to-face, and cut out the pattern, making two copies.

2. For the top ruffle: Fold the purple strip lengthwise, and sew across each folded end. Turn the seams inside, fold lengthwise, and sew a gathering thread along the raw edges. Pull the thread to gather the strip into a 7" ruffle. Align the ruffle's raw edge to the stocking top edge, pin ¼" from each end, and sew.

3. Match the lining and stocking face-to-face with the ruffle tucked in. Sew across the top, on the ruffle stitch line. Open the seam, and fold the ruffle upward.

The lining and top fabric can all be cut in one piece and then cut in half to insert the purple ruffle at the stocking top.

4. Lay the red/gold ribbon across the stocking, ¼" from the ruffle. Top stitch the top edge to the stocking.

5. Press a hem in the copper fabric, and lay it across the stocking with the raw top edge tucked under the red/gold ribbon ½". Top stitch across the red ribbon, including the copper in the seam.

6. Lay the gold lace so it overlaps the copper hem, and top stitch across the top and bottom edges.

7. Align the green ribbon down ⅜" from this seam, and sew across on both edges.

8. Fold the stocking lengthwise, stocking-to-stocking and lining-to-lining. Tuck the ruffle ends out of the seam, and sew from fabric heel to lining heel, stopping 3" from the end. Turn it through this opening in the heel, and stuff the toe. Sew the lining closed, and tuck it into the stocking.

9. Hand sew the bells and any other embellishments onto the stocking.

10. Pinch and knot the green ribbon into a bow 4" across with a loop to hang. Sew the bow on the stocking.

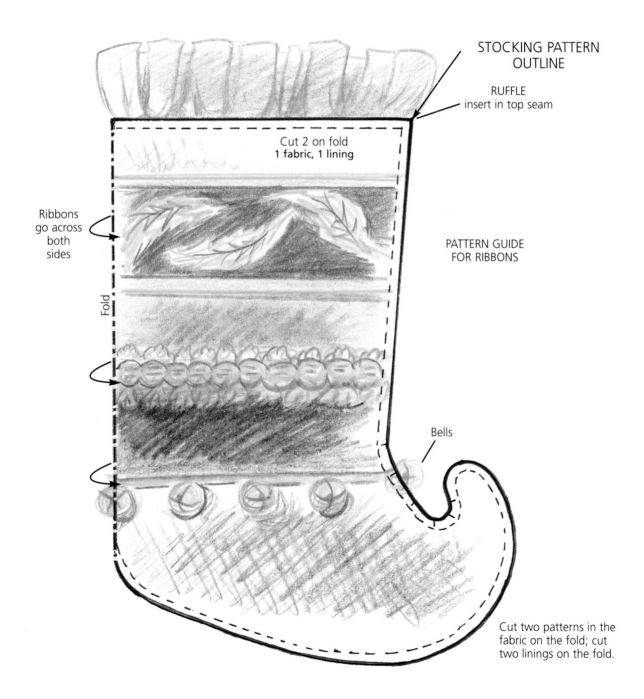

STOCKING PATTERN OUTLINE

RUFFLE
insert in top seam

Cut 2 on fold
1 fabric, 1 lining

Ribbons go across both sides

Fold

PATTERN GUIDE FOR RIBBONS

Bells

Cut two patterns in the fabric on the fold; cut two linings on the fold.

7 Snowman

DESIGNED BY IRIS VAN BUREN

This cheerful snowman made of non-melting materials will last through warm summers in your Christmas ornament box.

YOU NEED

- Hat: 3" x 6" blue felt, 3" x 6" green felt, 1" green pom-pom
- Scarf: 2" x 16" blue felt, green scraps
- 2 white 3" polystyrene balls
- 2 black 12" chenille stems
- 4" black fine wire
- ¼" round stick
- 1" red pom-pom
- 4 black ¼" pom-poms
- Snow (shredded plastic available seasonally at Michaels craft stores)
- Scissors, glue gun or Sobo® glue, pliers

*A*merican Christmas memories commonly feature a northern scene with evergreen trees in snowy fields and Santa riding his sleigh, a vehicle clearly limited to snow or the Milky Way. Snow enchants us because it transforms a landscape, smoothing familiar sights into mysterious mounds and chilling the air to crispness. And, when it is just the right temperature, warm moist snow will pack and you can make a snowman. Like the mythical Santa, snowmen come alive in imagination. Think of the song *Frosty the Snowman*.

Various white materials can be used to simulate snow for a movie scene shot in the summer, or to make a snowman that will last until next Christmas and beyond.

1. Coat the balls with Sobo glue, and roll them in the shredded plastic snow.

2. To join the balls firmly together, push the skewer into the head, glue the joint, and push the skewer into the body.

3. Trace the pattern, and cut out one scarf and four hat pieces. Sew the hat pieces together, and turn them right side out. Glue the hat on the snowman's head, the hatband to the hat, and the red pom-pom to the top of the hat.

4. To make each arm, clip a stem into three 4" pieces. Twist the pieces together at one end. Shape the loose ends into a branch. Poke a hole in the side of the body, glue, and push the arm's twisted end into the body. Repeat for the other arm.

5. Glue the scarf neck on the back side, and wrap it firmly around the neck, leaving one end downward and the other end over the shoulder. Glue the trim on the hat and scarf. Glue on the pom-pom nose, eyes, and buttons.

6. Follow the pattern to bend the wire into a crinkly mouth. Bend the wire ends inward, put glue on the wire ends, stick the ends into the head, and press the mouth in place.

7. To hang, thread beads on a wire, twist one end of the wire into a hook, and push the other end into the snowman's head. Or sew a thread into his hat for hanging.

SCARF

CHENILLE STEM ARMS
Make 2

Insert

Cut 1 on
fold

Cut 18

Cut 12
6 green
6 blue

HAT

Cut 4
2 blue
2 green

Pom poms

Bend
end to
insert

Wire mouth

SNOWMAN
PATTERN

HAT BAND Cut 1 on fold

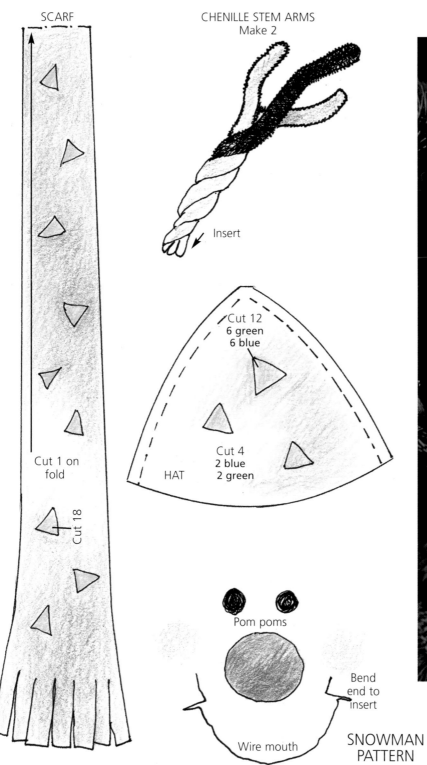

19

8 Dog Star

Keep a favorite pet forever by modeling him into an ornament to hang on your Christmas tree; or let it dangle from your desk lamp all year long.

YOU NEED

- Papier-mâché*
- 2" wooden star
- 1" x 1" leather
- Silver glitter
- 8" gold cord
- Acrylic paint, white, brown, black
- Artist's paintbrush, glue, scissors, sandpaper

Celluclay® (Activa Products) is dry and ready to mix. Creative Paperclay® comes ready to model. Both are available at Michaels stores.

$\mathcal{A}$nimals play their part in Christmas, whether pulling Santa's sleigh, gathering to observe the newborn babe, or as models for ornaments. Kathy Flory, who designed this ornament, says she takes pictures of animals in various poses to guide her in modeling her realistic subjects. She prefers natural poses, such as the way a particular dog sits to one side or angles his head. This careful observation helps her show the animal's personality. After a friend's dog died, Kathy sculpted the little fellow with a tiny halo and wings, his head turned to look back soulfully.

This dog is a feisty, persistent creature. He catches his star and hangs on, prompting his name, Frisbee, painted on his collar. Make this dog, or try sculpting your own pet.

1. Study various poses of the pet for the basic shapes. This dog consists of a pear shape for the body, a smaller pear shape for the head, "ham" shapes for the back legs, and rolls for front legs.

2. Assemble the basic parts of the dog, and stick the papier-mâché pieces firmly together. You can model over a wire armature or add strips of wet paper to hold the shapes together.

3. Once you have the correct proportions, model the distinct characteristics of the animal's personality. You know this persistent little beagle would never let go of your rag even if you spun him around.

4. Once the papier-mâché is dry, sand off any rough spots. Use white, black, and brown acrylic paint for his fur, spots, and collar. Paint his name, Frisbee, on the collar.

5. Cut out the leather ear shapes, and glue them on.

6. Paint the star with glue, and sprinkle on the glitter.

7. Glue the dog's mouth firmly to the star. Attach a cord to the star for hanging.

> $\mathcal{T}$ip   To make your own papier-mâché, tear paper into tiny bits, soak them in water, wring them dry, and add glue.

The star on top of your Christmas tree symbolizes the celestial event the Magi followed to attend the newborn Jesus in Bethlehem. Astronomers, theists, and storytellers all try to explain this phenomenon. No wonder. The stars and the heavens have intrigued people since time began. They guide the way for voyagers, help astrologers tell your fortune, and light up the night for all of us. Children chant, "Star light, star bright, first star I see tonight. Wish I may, wish I might, have the wish I wish tonight." It's probably the planet Venus they see. Planets shine but stars twinkle.

This star radiates beams, representing the Christmas star.

1. To make the 7½" background bow, thread the wire across one end of the wide ribbon. This end becomes the center of the bow. Finger pleat the wire ribbon every 8", and thread the wire through the centers for 4" loops. Twist the wire around the center of the completed bow and back to the front. For an inch from the center of the bow, glue the edge of each loop to the edge of the next loop,

2. Place three gold and three white stems across the center, and wire them together in place.

3. Thread three or four craft beads on each of the gold stems. Add a gold loop, and fold over the tip of the gold stem ½" to secure the loop. Space and glue each gold stem to the center of each bow loop.

4. Thread one pearl on the tip of each white stem. Twist the middle twice around a pencil to make a spiral.

5. Twist the fourth gold stem around the pencil ten times, and twist the ends together to form a circle. Thread the wire through the large bead and over the stem circle. Twist both wire ends to the back. Twist them together three times, and glue. Use this to wire the star to the treetop.

You Need

- 48" x 2½" sheer embroidered gold ribbon*
- 4 metallic gold chenille stems 12" x 6mm glitter chenille stem
- 3 iridescent white stems 12" x 6mm*
- 24 multicolored ⅜" plastic craft beads*
- 6½" gold beaded loops
- 6 cream 8mm pearls*
- ½" knobby white bead
- 10" wire
- Glue gun, pencil

Used in this project: ribbon from Michaels, item No.XA175/25-100; beads from Darice® Craft Designer.

10 Goldfish

*F*ish are early Christian symbols. Along with loaves of bread, they were the most common sustenance at the time. And in some places, such as the Midwest on Friday nights, times haven't changed that much as to what we eat.

Fish also serve as household pets. Goldfish in particular have been popular in China and Japan for centuries. Over the years, more and more exotic colors and shapes were developed. They make delightful and ornamental pets. You can have one fish in a fairly small aquarium. They don't mind living alone, where they don't have to compete for food, space, or attention. Fish, by their compact design, bright colors, and exotic shapes, make ideal ornament imagery.

Fish come in such a spectrum. You can sew a soft sculptured fish in many colors and many fabrics.

YOU NEED

- 6" x 8" piece of metallic fabric
- 10" x 8" edging of lace
- Two ½" beads
- Two ⅜" eyes with post and washer
- One ⅜" ring bead for the mouth
- Sewing machine, scissors, paper, glue, needle, and thread

1. For the lace fish, trace the pattern as is, or trace it on folded paper for a whole pattern. Trace the fin pattern.

2. Cut out the lace (whole pattern), aligning the lace edge on the tail. For a lace fin, align the fin pattern with the design in the lace that looks like a fin, and cut out.

3. Metallic fabric ravels, so sew and cut it out this way: align the pattern on the lace, lay both the pattern and the lace on the uncut metallic fabric, and pin. Sew through the pattern on the stitch line around the metallic body from (A) to (C). The pattern stabilizes the fragile fabrics. Carefully tear away the paper pattern. Do the same for the fin, if it will be lined with gold.

4. Trim the fabric just outside the stitch line.

5. Place the fin on the fish body with the round tip upward. Align the raw edges (D) to (E). Fold the fish along the back center line, and sew on the stitch line from (A) to (B), leaving the tail open for stuffing the body. Turn right side out.

NOTE: *For the silk fish, trace the pattern, dye paint the fabric, set the color, and proceed as above minus the lining fabric.*

6. Cut a ¹⁄₁₆" hole for the eye post. Put the washers inside the fish. Add a bead to the post, insert the eye post through the fish fabric into the washer. Push firmly to secure. Repeat for the other eye.

7. Push fiberfill stuffing into the body through the tail. Sew or glue the mouth bead on. Sew on a string to hang.

Kittens, reindeer, bears, and other animals, such as this dye-painted silk fish, make delightful ornaments for the tree.

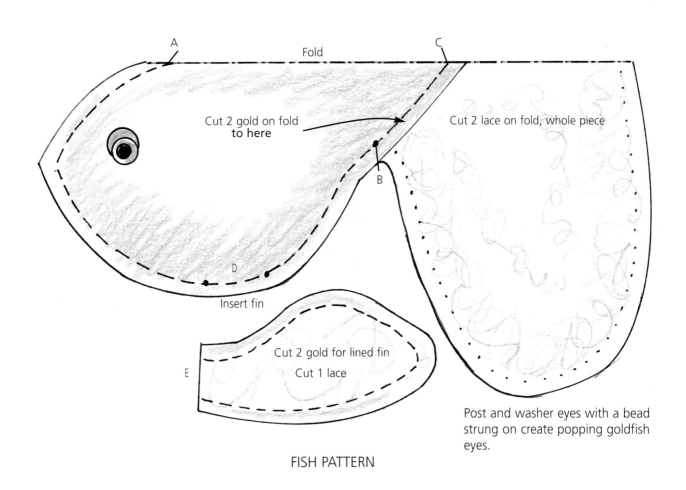

A   Fold   C

Cut 2 gold on fold
to here

Cut 2 lace on fold, whole piece

B

D

Insert fin

E   Cut 2 gold for lined fin

Cut 1 lace

Post and washer eyes with a bead strung on create popping goldfish eyes.

FISH PATTERN

11 Gingerbread House

"Lebkuckenhaeusel" or "house for nibbling at" is the German name for a gingerbread house. This tiny gingerbread-style house is not edible.

$\mathcal{F}$oods shaped into Christmas imagery include: gingerbread houses, gingerbread cookie men, candy canes, and ribbon candy. Gingerbread has been baked in Europe for centuries, possibly introduced by the returning Crusaders. Ginger flavors and preserves the food.

Nuremberg, Germany, over the years known as the gingerbread capital of the world, attracted many artisans who contributed to the most beautiful cakes in Europe. Large pieces of lebkuken were baked into "witches houses" as in the Hansel and Gretel fairy tale. These cakes were called lebkuckenhaeusel, meaning "houses for nibbling at." Gingerbread houses caught on in America both in architecture and Christmas baking. Many, from kids to cooks, enjoy making richly decorated, ornamented gingerbread houses in styles from cottages to castles to elaborate Victorian houses.

You need

- 3" x 15" brown mat board (the reverse side is white)
- 24" x ⅛" metallic gold ribbon
- 5 red heart beads
- 6 green ½" disks (polymer clay or bead)
- 2 strands of rose-colored ⅜" bugle beads
- Plastic beads: assorted pearls in sizes from 4mm to 7mm, pearls in pastel colors, ⅜" gold rings, 3mm metallic beads, ¼" red and green sequins
- Glue gun with beading glue sticks, tweezers, large-hole needle, utility knife, paper cutter or scissors

1. Cut the mat board into one base, 3" square; two sides, 1¼" x 2¾"; two roofs 2" x 2¾"; and two front/backs 2¾ x 3" with a roof peak, according to the pattern.

2. Glue the sides to the front and back, brown sides outward. Glue the bottom edges to the base to stabilize the square. Glue the roof, white sides upward, to the top edges.

Gluing Tips

- To glue on a row of beads, keep them strung or insert a wire. Glue the row in place, and then remove the string or wire.
- To glue on sequins or small beads, use tweezers to keep the glue off your hands.
- Practice with the glue gun to avoid glue "strings" by touching the tip to the background. Pick off glue strings with the tweezers.
- Avoid gobs of glue by running a smooth straight line.

3. Glue on the beads as shown, or in any pattern you wish. For ideas, look on the Internet for Gingerbread houses and beads.

4. Glue on the doorway gold ribbon and then the base ribbon.

5. Glue the hanging ribbon to the center of the roof peak. Glue on the top row of green beads.

GINGERBREAD HOUSE PATTERN

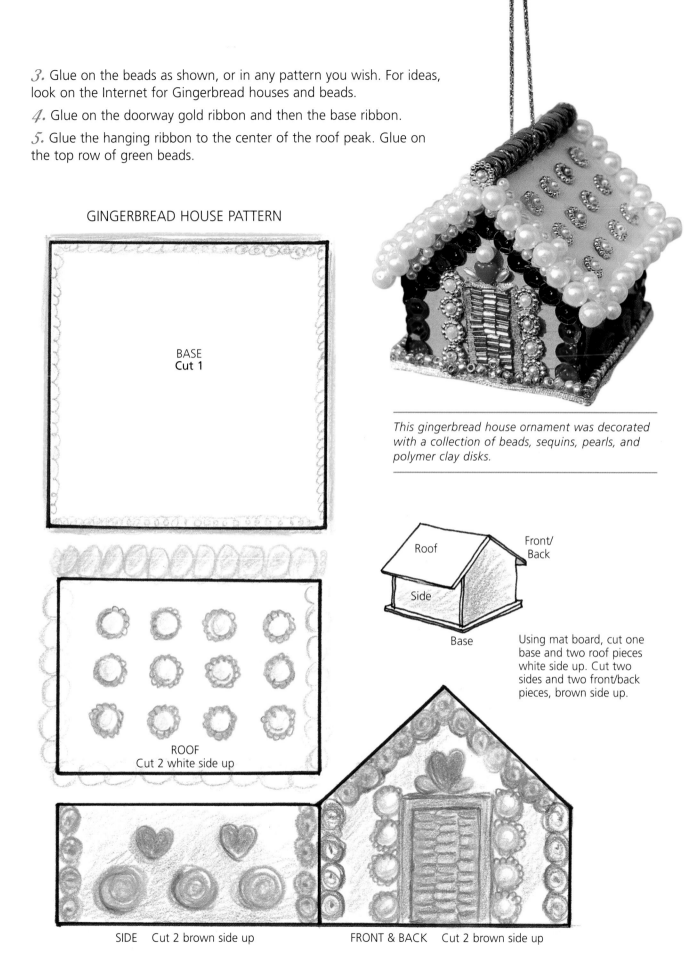

This gingerbread house ornament was decorated with a collection of beads, sequins, pearls, and polymer clay disks.

BASE
Cut 1

Roof

Front/Back

Side

Base

Using mat board, cut one base and two roof pieces white side up. Cut two sides and two front/back pieces, brown side up.

ROOF
Cut 2 white side up

SIDE   Cut 2 brown side up

FRONT & BACK   Cut 2 brown side up

12 Christmas Red and Green

DESIGNED BY LESLIE MASTERS

Color combinations, like sounds or musical notes, trigger images within us. Orange and black bring to mind Halloween, while red and green symbolize Christmas. These complimentary color opposites appear in the many plants available at Yuletide. The holly plant has waxy dark green leaves and bright red berries. Poinsettias, common to Southern climes, have large green leaves and bright red bracts. In Germany, red apples were hung from the early Christian Paradise Tree. In our homes, dark green evergreen boughs are tied with vibrant red bows to proclaim the season. Sounds limiting? New poinsettia varieties come in a range of colors from lemony white to clear or speckled pink to deep red. And consider the endless shades of red and green you can use to make ornaments and decorate your home.

Red and green may symbolize the Yuletide, but in reality Christmas brings to mind a dazzling array of colors in gift wrappings, foods, toys, decorations, and ornaments.

Four traditional Christmas images by Leslie Masters (and a teddy bear by the author) show some of the range of Shrinky Dinks ornament possibilities.

1. Photocopy the pattern. Trace it on the frosty side of the Shrinky Dinks plastic sheet.

2. Color in the designs with wax-based pencils, shading and blending the colors.

3. Cut out the shapes. Use manicure scissors for detailed cutting. Use a paper punch for the ribbon hole. Baking shrinks the ornament to ⅓ its size, so punch several times to make a larger hole.

4. Preheat a toaster or conventional oven to 325 degrees. Line a tray with paper, place the Shrinky Dinks pieces on it, and put it into the preheated oven. Objects will curl during baking. Bake 1 to 3 minutes plus 30 seconds until they flatten.

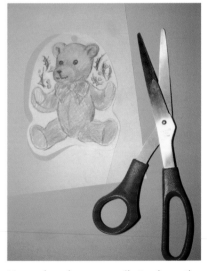

Use colored wax pencils to draw the image on the frosty side of the plastic sheet, punch a hole in the top, and then cut out around it.

YOU NEED

- 1 sheet Shrinky Dinks*
- 6" x ¼" ribbon for each ornament
- Wax pencils, manicure scissors, regular scissors, hole punch, brown paper, oven

*Used in this project: Frosted Ruff 'N Ready Shrinky Dinks® from K& B Innovations.

5. Remove the pieces from the oven, press flat while cooling (15 seconds), or shape the piece over an object within the first 10 seconds. Handle carefully. They are hot.

6. Tie a ribbon through the hole at the top to hang.

The baked teddy bear ornament shrinks to a third of its original size, as shown when placed in its cut out hole in the plastic shown on the previous page.

Tip Watercolors will smear on Shrinky Dinks. To apply color, use wax-based colored pencils (Berol® Eagle Colors, Prismacolor®, or Faber Castell®) or a thin coat of acrylic paint, which dries waterproof.

Trace design on this line **and cut out** after coloring

PATTERNS

Photocopy at 300%. The design will shrink to 1/3 its size.

Two more Shrinky Dinks by Leslie Masters sparkle with added glitter. Tie a ribbon through the hole and add a hook to hang.

13 Old-Fashioned Sled

Designer unknown

Little wooden sled ornaments remind older folk of their snowy rides down the long ago hills.

Sleds come in many forms—wooden with steel runners, molded plastic pallets, long toboggans for several riders, or horse-drawn sleighs. Santa arrives in his sleigh pulled by eight tiny reindeer, a scene popularized in the Christmas poem *The Night Before Christmas*. In earlier times, one sturdy reindeer pulled Santa's sleigh. In Spain, he arrives by boat, and elsewhere he comes on a white horse. Eventually you discover that Mom and Dad deliver the gifts in the family car, and one of these presents might be a sled.

1. Shape the sled pieces. Sled top: One uncut 4½" stick; two 3⅜" sticks, round at one end and cut angled 45 degrees across the other end. Handle: One 1¾" stick, rounded at each end. Runners: Two 4¼" sticks, ends cut 45 degrees downward at one end and upward on the other end. Braces: Two 1" pieces.

2. Drill small holes on the handle, ¼" from each end.

3. Glue the upright braces to the upright runners, 1" from the rear and 1½" from the front.

4. Glue the center top stick to the braces, lined up with the runners. Glue the side top pieces to the braces, ⅛" from the center piece and ¼" in from the rear.

5. Glue the handle to the center top stick, centered ¼" from the end.

6. Decorate the sled with acrylic paint or use a permanent marker to inscribe a name. Varnish with polyurethane.

7. Poke the cord ends down through the handle holes, and knot.

YOU NEED

- Seven ⅜" crafts sticks (with rounded ends)
- 6" gold cord
- Acrylic paint, varnish
- Glue gun, sandpaper or emery board, drill and small bit, utility knife or sturdy scissors

Tip The wooden craft sticks, made of soft pine, can be cut with an X-Acto® or utility knife, sharp scissors, or a chopper-style paper cutter.

FOR THE LARGE SLED

Use 1" x 6" sticks to make the same pieces as above, in proportion. Trim the top side pieces to 4⅜" (angled) and the handle to 3-1/4" (both ends round). Make braces 1½" long. Make angled cuts on both ends of the runners, in opposite directions.

Half a century ago, ornaments for Christmas trees consisted of little more than a string of lights, tinsel, glass balls, and a few molded glass shapes imported from Europe. Kurt Adler, a European native, decided to bring a wider variety to America. He started an import business, gathering such ornaments as German angels, candy-container snowmen and Santas, Czechoslovakian spun glass ornaments, and Italian miniature tree lights. He has been bringing new ideas ever since—realistic artificial trees, snow domes with lively scenes, and nut-cracker toys in a variety of characters. Lately he has imported Polish blown glass ornaments in every possible theme, and mixed-media Santas of papier-mâché, fabric, faux gemstones, and jewelry. Other importers also bring us an aston-ishing variety of ornaments from around the world, but even with this variety and all the new innovations, balls remain the favorite tree ornaments.

This quick and easy ornament has a big punch with glued-on sequin stars and two ribbons.

1. Using the glue gun or Sobo glue, put a line of glue around the "equator" of the ball, and sprinkle on the gold stars. Quickly arrange the stars before the glue dries.

2. Clip the red ribbon into three 5" sections, angled at the tips. Twist the end of the 6" wire onto the wire loop at the top of the orna-ment. Thread each ribbon center on the wire. Evenly space the rib-bons, and glue them to the ornament loop.

3. Thread the wire through the white ribbon every four inches, twist-ing it face side down for each loop. Use the glue gun to secure each loop, and compress the loops on the wire to make a chrysanthemum bow.

4. Bend the wire into a hook at the top.

YOU NEED

- 3" glass or plastic ball
- Packet of ¼" gold stars
- 15" x 1" red and gold wire-edged ribbon
- 3 yards ½" white (iridescent) ribbon
- 6" wire
- Glue gun, scissors

15 Woven Ball

Crafters have a variety of fibers and techniques at hand for making ornaments. Ribbons, cords, yarns, and threads can be woven, knitted, crocheted, wrapped, and tied into round or shaped balls. The off-the-loom weaving technique used in this ball can be made with ribbons in a variety of widths, thicknesses, and a choice of coordinated colors for both the warp and weft. The ribbons are first woven into a flat mat, and then cut into shapes and fitted onto the polystyrene ball.

Or for a simpler ornament, fold the ribbon mat in half. Sew around the edges, leaving an opening to turn. Turn and sew the opening closed. Sew ribbon bows on the corners and a ribbon to hang.

Ribbons woven into a rectangle make a pillow-like ornament, enlivened with bows on the corners. Designer unknown.

1. Ribbon pieces: Cut 11 ribbon pieces 12" long out of assorted white, blue, gold, and red. Cut 24 pieces 6" long out of assorted white, blue, and gold ribbon, and red and blue gimp.

2. To hold the ribbons during weaving, make a 12" x 6" frame of masking tape on a flat surface, sticky side up with the corners taped down.

You need

- 3" polystyrene ball
- 48" x ⅜" white ribbon
- 48" x ⅜" blue ribbon
- 48" x ⅜" metallic gold ribbon
- 48" x ⅝" red ribbon
- 48" x ½" medium blue gimp
- 48" x ½" dark red gimp
- 45" x 1" red ribbon with gold stars
- 6" wire
- Masking tape, pencil, glue gun, sewing machine, scissors

Four elliptical shapes are cut from a woven ribbon rectangle. Each shape was machine stitched as shown to hold the edges and then glued on the plastic ball.

3. To weave: Arrange the short ribbons side by side along the top tape, and stick the ends to the tape. Beginning at the top left, stick the end of a long ribbon to the tape, and weave the ribbon over and under across the short ribbons, and then stick it down. Continue to weave the long ribbons across, alternating over and under.

4. Add tape over the sticky masking tape at the edges of the completed weaving (or it will stick to the sewing machine).

5. Cut out four pieces of the pattern, place them in a row on the weaving at 45-degree angles, and trace each.

6. Machine sew 1/16" inside the trace lines with short stitches. Cut out each section on the trace line.

7. Push the wire into the ball. Glue along the edges of one woven section, place the tip at the base of the wire, and press it firmly to the ball. Cup the ball in your hand to make the curve fit snugly. Repeat for each section until the ball is covered.

8. Clip the ends of the red star ribbon at an angle. Finger pinch the ribbon every 5" to make a fan-shaped bow. Twist the wire around the center of the bow, and form a hook at the end to hang.

Ribbons woven together cover a basic polystyrene ball for a festive effect.

Cut 4 from the woven ribbon piece

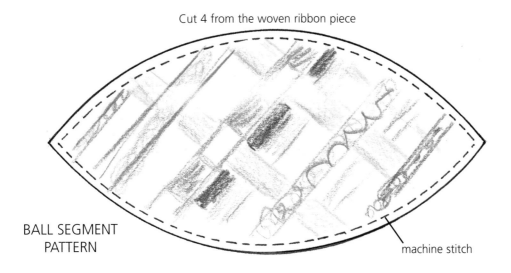

BALL SEGMENT
PATTERN

machine stitch

16 Japanese Temari Ball

DESIGNED BY LESLIE MASTERS

*E*very country and group of people creates some kind of ornament to decorate their homes or themselves. People in Japan and throughout Southeast Asia make traditional Temari balls. Originally, to while away the time, ladies of the court made the balls from sweet-smelling herbs encased in silken threads. Later the inside balls were formed by wrapping silk fabric round and round, but skilled hands were needed to form a perfect ball. Now silk, cotton, rayon, or metallic threads are wrapped around polystyrene balls. These materials for wrapping balls are readily available to anyone. Temari designs look complicated, but they are based on geometric point-by-point steps to create the pattern.

Popular Southeast Asian Temari balls have elaborate geometric designs created by wrapping colorful threads around a ball shape.

YOU NEED

- 2½" or 3" polystyrene ball
- 325 yards of sewing thread (cones are cheapest)
- A selection of colored threads, metallic threads, and embroidery threads
- 10 or more 1" variegated-color plastic head pins
- Darning needle, strips of paper, scissors

1. To prepare the ball, wrap it firmly and evenly with sewing thread until the entire ball is solidly covered. This hides the plastic surface and forms a base for stitching the pattern.

2. To plot the points for the guide pins:

a. Wrap a strip of paper around the widest part of the ball until it overlaps, and punch a pin through both ends. Fold the marked strip in half, pin hole to pin hole. Pin the strip to the ball at one end (A), and mark a pin at the other end (B) for the top and bottom points.

	divide strip in half
Strip	fold

Cover the ball with threads, and then make measured guidelines for accurate placement of the decorator threads to be added.

b. Again, fold the strip evenly, matching (A) to (B), and pin beside the fold at (C). Rotate the strip on (A), and place pins all around at several point (C)s.

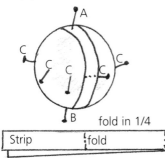

fold in 1/4

Strip	fold

c. Remove the strip, and fold it into eight even sections. Wrap it around at the (C) pins, and pin different colored pins at each fold. Remove the (C) pins.

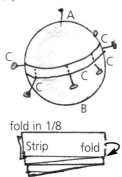

fold in 1/8

Strip   fold

3. For guide threads, thread the needle with a colored thread that measures eight times the circumference of the ball. Secure the thread, and wrap it from (A) to (B), touching a (C) pin. Wrap past each (C) pin to section the ball into eight "slices." Take the thread from (A) to (C), and wrap it around at (C). Remove the pins.

4. The pattern threads are herringbone stitched around the guide threads in various patterns. For a variety of designs and how to create your own, see *The Temari Book* by Anna Diamond.

The long thread is herringbone-stitched over the guidelines to make patterns. The basic first wrap still shows.

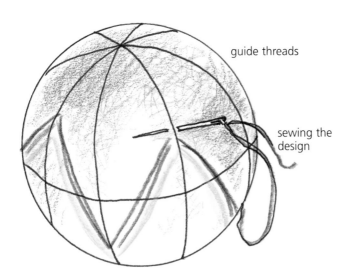

guide threads

sewing the design

A completed ball made with lustrous and metallic threads results in an elaborate eight-point design.

Beaded Ball

Nothing comes to mind more quickly than jewels and beads when thinking about decorations. Beads come in an amazing variety of materials—glass, crystal, semiprecious gemstones, gold, silver, brass, paper, polymer clay, wire, and all manner of plastic. They are made into endless shapes, requiring only a hole for stringing.

The two kinds of beadwork are woven and sewn. Woven beadwork is created on a beadwork loom with orderly rows of same size beads woven into the warp threads. In sewn beadwork, the beads are attached to a piece of fabric, which allows for a variety of sizes and kinds of beads. Beads can be sewn on one at a time or strung in groups of three or four and then fastened as a group. Beads of various shapes and sizes may be used and placed on the fabric randomly, solidly, or in patterns with the fabric exposed.

Beadwork has been practiced around the world since ancient times, especially in parts of Africa and Asia. The American Indians are also noted for their beadwork. Two currently popular varieties of strung beads are lamp work glass beads and Austrian Crystal beads.

This flat beadwork is a portrait of an ornament sewn with tiny beads. Also shown are plastic apples.

YOU NEED

- 3½" x 4" stiff white fabric (buckram)
- 3½" x 4" felt backing in a harmonizing color
- 2mm beads: (amounts are approximate) 300 light blue, 250 light green, 200 dark green, 200 orange, 150 red, 25 clear pink, 50 clear white
- 3mm beads: 150 gold
- Bugle beads: 50 gold, 15 green
- Beading or small needle, beading thread, 3H pencil, scissors

1. Using the photo on the following page as a pattern, trace the design on the buckram with a 3H pencil (hard lead does not smear).

2. You can sew each bead on individually or "couch" them on. Sewing each bead separately makes the strongest result. To couch beads on, secure the thread to the buckram and sew a string of beads. At the end of the string, insert the needle to the back. Sew up between one to three beads on the string to catch the thread and sew back through the same hole to couch the beads in place. Repeat every two or three beads along the strung beads on the pattern lines. Sew a firm knot when the thread runs out.

3. Begin by sewing the gold bugle beads across the center. Sew the green seed beads along the edge of the gold.

4. Sew on the blue beads from the outside edge inward. Sew on the gold edging last. You can secure the threads by spreading glue on the back side of the buckram.

5. Cut the felt to size. Sew a hem on the base fabric, and cover it with the felt. Sew (or glue) around the edge to secure.

BALL PATTERN

CROSS SECTIONS

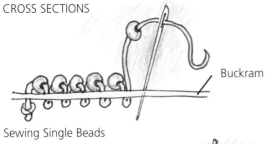

Buckram

Sewing Single Beads

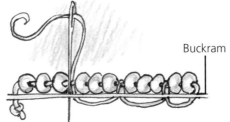

Buckram

Couching a string of beads

Tip A quick method to apply beads is to glue the beads onto the buckram. To keep the beads in place, string the beads on the thread, place the glue on the buckram and lay the beads on the glue.

Imagine the mix of piney evergreen and the scent of cloves and oranges from a pomander ball wafting from your Christmas tree.

You need

- 3 oz. (or more) whole dried cloves
- ½"-wide heavy dark red gimp
- 15" x 2" metallic gold polka dot ribbon
- Soft green tassel and cord
- 4" florist wire
- Skewer, glue gun, pencil, scissors

*C*hestnuts roasting on an open fire. Popcorn popping. Spices flavoring the air. Feasting is an important part of Christmas with appealing tastes and smells of the season. Different countries serve their favorites: spicy wassail in England, glogg in Sweden, or egg nog in the United States. You can almost smell Dickens' Christmas goose in England, taste the fruit and nut filled stollen bread in Germany, or savor the cake called buche de Noel in France.

Food as a gift includes the invention of the fruitcake, soaked in rum or bourbon to preserve it, and then sent from a kitchen in England to expatriates serving in India. Food as decoration means candy canes, cookies, and nuts tied onto the Christmas tree. Food for scent includes pomander balls, made in earlier times to ward off illness. In later times, people put them in cupboards and drawers for fresh fragrance. A spiced orange will keep its aroma for a year or more as it dries.

1. Begin with a large fresh orange with the skin tender enough to pierce. Wrap the ribbon around the orange from top to bottom. Twist the ribbon at the base of the orange, and pull it to the top, segmenting the orange in four. Mark the ribbon edges with a pencil and remove it.

2. Use a skewer to pierce holes about ¼" apart for the cloves. Punch in the dried clove tips to fill the entire skin, leaving the track for the ribbons. (Or fill the entire ball, and then tie on the ribbons.) Let it dry a week to shrink.

3. Wrap the red gimp tightly around the ball in the open tracks, and glue it in place.

4. Glue the green cord over the gimp with the tassel at the bottom, and make a hanging loop at the top.

5. Finger pinch the 2" ribbon in the center of 6" lengths so it forms a fan. Wire the ribbon to the hanging cord. Clip the ends of the ribbon at an angle.

In early times, paintings embellished the walls in churches, not only for beauty but also to tell the religious story. Some of the magical aspects of the Christian religion were hard to picture. Who knew what cherubim and angels looked like? So artists created images for them, and none were more appealing than fat little cherubim. They cluster in the skies of many paintings doing their good works. These traditional images are now popular in many additional art forms—sculptured in wood, stone, fabric, ceramic, glass, and more.

Sculpey, the polymer modeling clay used for this cherub, comes in a rich assortment of colors. You can also mix them like paint to make your own colors.

1. For the body, roll a tube of polymer clay ¾" round by 1½" long. For arms and legs, roll four 1¼" tubes. For the head, roll a 1 " ball.

2. Twist a wire in half, making a loop at the top. Push the twisted ends through the top of the head into the body.

3. Bend the leg tube at the knee, and shape the foot. Press the leg firmly onto the lower end of the body, and smooth the hip. Repeat for the other leg.

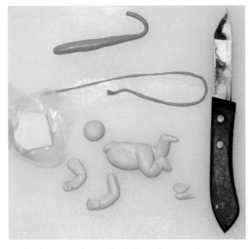

Roll plump tubes of pink polymer clay to make this chubby cherub. Trim the clay with kitchen or clay tools.

4. Bend the arms at the elbows, and curl the ends into simple hand shapes. Press the arms firmly onto the body, and smooth at the shoulders.

5. For hair, roll a long skinny string of gold-colored clay, cut it in ¾" pieces, and roll tiny spirals. Stick the spirals to the head (around the wire loop) overlapping each other. Poke eyes and a mouth with the skewer. Roll a tiny ball for the nose.

6. Shape triangular white wings, and stick them firmly on the cherub's back.

7. Cut the gold ribbon in half. Tie one half into a bow on the wire loop. Tie the other half around the center of the bow. Knot and tie the ends together to hang the ornament.

YOU NEED

- Polymer clay*, white, gold, flesh color
- Wire
- 15" x ³⁄₁₆" gold wire-edged ribbon
- Knife, skewer, oven

*Used in this project: Sculpey® brand modeling compound.

20 Angel

DESIGNED BY BROOKE GREESON

The story of Christmas comes mainly from the Gospels of Saint Luke and Saint Matthew in the New Testament. The story tells how an angel appeared to the shepherds outside the town of Bethlehem to tell them of Jesus' birth. The wise men, called magi, followed the bright star that led them to the birthplace. Angels are pure spirits who carry out heavenly duties. The word angel comes from Greek meaning messenger. Painters through the ages have pictured angels in various forms, usually floating above as they carry out their missions. The Catholic Church lists the order of angels with Seraphim first. Next come Cherubim, Thrones, Dominions, Virtues, Powers, Principalities (considered hostile to man), Archangels, and Angels.

The good news is every one of us has a guardian angel.

Hovering just over your head could be your own guardian angel. This tiny one guards the Christmas tree.

You Need

- 4" x 6" white satin
- 3" x 4" pink satin
- Wood clay, papier-mâché, or polymer clay
- Yellow yarn
- Fiberfill
- Skewer, sewing machine, scissors, needle, and thread

1. Using the clay, model the legs with feet to measure 1¾" so that ½" of the leg goes into the dress. Make the head stretched forward on a ¾" neck. Model a nose and stick it on. Use a skewer to poke eyes and a mouth. Make the hands and arms 1¾" long. Bake the pieces.

2. To make the dress, trace the pattern on fabric with the sleeve cuff on the selvage edge. Cut out the dress and wings. By sewing machine, sew the dress back seam, and then join the round base to the dress. Cut ⅛" holes for the feet. Sew the wings. Turn these pieces.

3. To assemble the angel, fold the dress neck edge into the body, and stuff the body with fiberfill. Put glue on the top end of the legs, and push them into the dress leg holes and into the stuffing. Put glue on the bottom of the neck, and push it into the neck hole.

4. Glue the wrist lightly, wrap the sleeve around it, and hand sew the sleeve seam. Repeat for the other wrist. Sew the arms to the body. Stuff the wings, and hand sew them to the angel's back. Glue on the hair.

5. Make a loop with the thread, and sew it on the back of the angel to hang the ornament.

The sculptured angel and cherubim were hung before mirrors in the guest bath last year, and looked so good they were kept there permanently.

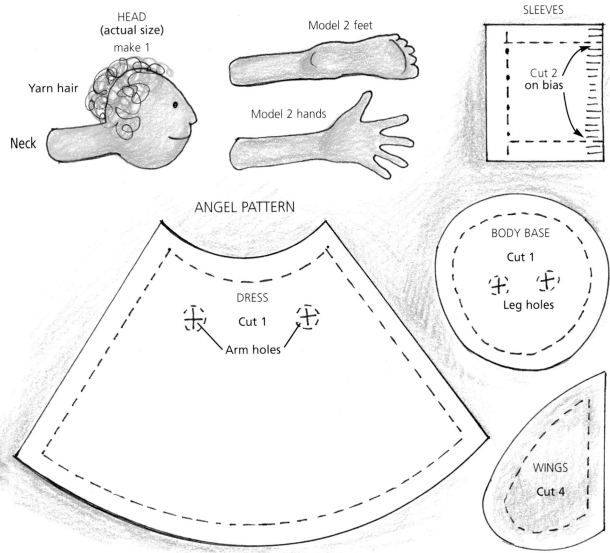

HEAD
(actual size)
make 1

Yarn hair

Neck

Model 2 feet

Model 2 hands

SLEEVES

Cut 2
on bias

ANGEL PATTERN

DRESS

Cut 1

Arm holes

BODY BASE

Cut 1

Leg holes

WINGS

Cut 4

The crèche symbolizes the religious aspect of Christmas more than any other icon. This scene depicts the birth of Christ in a stable, since there was no room at the inn. Crèches are designed in many forms and materials. The most modest are tiny wooden scenes with only the mother, father, and child. In warm climates, such as Mexico, scenes are made of clay, which more accurately portrays what might have been a cave in biblical days. Many cities have full size crèche scenes with animals, shepherds, and even wise men. No crèche rivals in drama the Radio City Music Hall scene with real people portraying the family, the shepherds, and the Magi, accompanied by real donkeys, sheep, and camels.

This small crèche, the holy family scene, measures 2¾" by 4¼" and can be made easily from thin wooden craft sticks.

You Need

- 3" square silver card stock
- Two ¾"-wide craft sticks (wide)*
- Three ⅜"-wide crafts sticks (narrow)*
- Two ⅜" wooden circles (faces)*
- ½" x 1½" oval wooden piece (baby)*
- 3" gold chenille stem
- 8" iridescent chenille stem
- 1½" gold metal star
- ⅜" gold circle bead (baby halo)
- 24" gold ribbon
- Utility knife, glue gun, permanent marking pen

*Used in this project: Forster® wood pieces.

1. Cut the background shape out of silver card stock.

2. Using narrow sticks, trim one stick to 2¾", rounded at both ends, for the base. Trim two narrow sticks to 1¾" for the sides.

3. Using the wide sticks, cut two 2½" roof pieces, each with one rounded end. For the figures, use wide sticks to cut one 2" stick and one 1¾" stick.

4. Glue the tall figure on the background with the base aligned at the bottom. Glue the star, point up, overlapping the tall figure. Glue the shorter figure on the star, base aligned with the bottom of the background. Glue the oval baby over both figures, angled toward the taller figure. Glue on the baby's halo bead, and then glue on the round faces.

5. Glue the base to the background and figures. Glue the sides to the background and base. Glue the roof pieces to the sides and background. Thread the gold ribbon through the roof joining before gluing the roof at the top.

6. Trim and shape the stems to fit into the stable and glue in place. Tie the gold ribbon in a bow, glue at the knot, and tie the long ends to hang.

Crèches appear at Christmas time as tiny tree ornaments, as more elaborate mantle scenes, and as full-sized models on church lawns.

CRÈCHE PATTERN

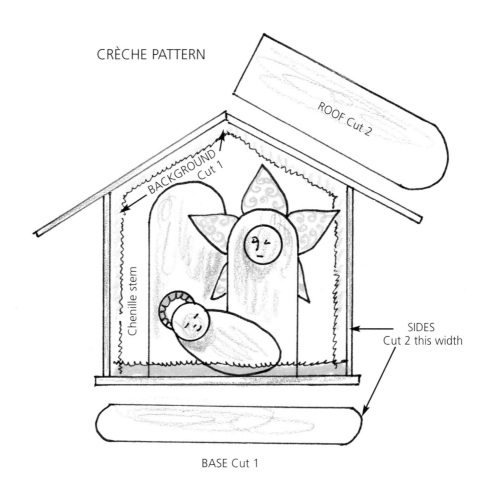

ROOF Cut 2

BACKGROUND Cut 1

Chenille stem

SIDES
Cut 2 this width

BASE Cut 1

Wreaths

For thousands of years, people have enjoyed decorating their homes with greenery to celebrate the fall harvest and the mid-winter New Year.

Wreaths can be made from many materials and hold significant meanings. Evergreens twisted into wreaths imply eternal life. Laurel leaf wreaths circled the heads of victors in early times. Wreaths of fruits and leaves carved in stone, fitted in mosaic, or painted were used to decorate many Italian homes and palaces, and they're still popular today. Evergreen Advent wreaths are made to hold five candles, one lit for each Sunday of the Yule season and a center one for Christmas.

You can make wreaths of leaves and fruit, ribbons, toys, ears of corn, pinecones, silk flowers, small toys, or whatever you have. Hang them on your door, lay them on holiday tables, or even wear them.

Add handmade ornaments to your front door wreath (purchased from grandson Bradley Stroud, Boy Scout).

This gold painted 30" wreath of branches and preserved holly leaves is strung with tiny white lights that cast a warm glow from its place on the family room wall.

1. Cut out a 3" diameter ring, ⅜"-wide with a 2¼" open center.

2. Tie the monofilament line around the ring and knot as a hanger.

Glue small seashells on a cutout ring base to make the shell wreath.

3. Using the hot glue gun, attach various seacoast shells—ceriths, periwinkles, and flat snails. Dab glue on the base. Press the shell's large end into the glue with the pointed end outward. The outer shells should project beyond the base and the inner ones toward the center. Fill the entire base.

4. Use two scallop shells fanned outward and two ceriths pointed inward for the ribbon. For a two-sided ornament, flip the base over and add more shells.

Use a glue gun to create a wreath of tiny seashells.

YOU NEED

- 60 dyed shells ½" to ¾" long (in packages at crafts stores)
- 3" diameter flat ring of plastic, cardboard, or wood
- 6" monofilament line
- Glue gun, scissors

The large conch and starfish show the tiny size of the small shell wreath.

23 Bell Wreath

1. String the bells on the wire, alternating sizes.

2. Bend the strung wire into a loop. Twist the ends of the wire together, leaving 2" of twisted wire at the top. Bend the wire into a hook.

3. Pinch the wide ribbon into a 3"-wide bow for the wreath top. Tie the narrow ribbon around the center of the pinch bow and the top of the wreath. Knot it and tie a bow.

Thread brass bells on a wire hoop and tie on a metallic ribbon for a festive 5" wreath.

You Need

- 11 brass ⅝" bells
- 15 brass ½" bells
- 9 brass ⅜" bells
- 18" x 1½" decorative wire-edged ribbon
- 18" x ⅛" gold ribbon
- 11" wire
- Wire clippers, scissors

Christmas Trees

*I*n the German medieval religious play, Adam and Eve met at the Paradise Tree, an evergreen hung with apples. This was the most likely forerunner of our decorated Christmas trees. Later tree trimmers added fruits, nuts, lighted candles, and paper roses. Now Christmas trees come with an endless variety of decorations, including lights, tinsel, blown glass ornaments, wooden toys, candy canes, molded plastic figures, and a star on top. A single theme tree might display only crystal ornaments and white lights, all kinds of teddy bears, or wooden ornaments. Popular now are elaborate baroque ornaments and wire ribbons, or trees that have been spray painted white, blue, or other colors.

Choosing a Christmas Tree

Years ago people surprised children with a fully-decorated tree on Christmas Eve, but now trees are bedecked for a month or more. It pays to choose a tree with good needle retention. The best real Christmas trees are Fraser, balsam, noble, Canaan, concord, or white firs. People love these for their beauty, shape, fragrance, and a needle retention of four to five weeks. Trees with a shorter needle life include Douglas fir, Scotch pine, and Eastern white pine (grown on Christmas tree farms). Beautiful as the blue spruce and white spruce are, they only last a week. Whatever kind you get, keep the trunk in water, and don't put burning candles on or near it.

Authentic-looking manufactured trees keep their needles forever and come in a variety of sizes, kinds, colors, and qualities. You can fold them up limb by limb to put away, or wrap the whole decorated tree in a plastic bag and store it for next year. The newest trees have built in lights.

Many people now have more than one tree, giving them more decorating possibilities in a variety of themes. New design ideas pop up each year.

The author's Christmas tree—the one that goes up and down stairs fully decorated every Christmas.

To fold this light-weight tree, start with a square of colored paper. Trim the tree with gold cord and sequins.

YOU NEED

- 2 colored 6" to 9" paper squares
- 6 to 12 beads
- 1½" gold metal star
- 24" gold cord
- Sequins in multiple shapes
- Heavy thread
- Cello tape, hole punch, needle, glue gun

1. With the right side facing down, bring the lower left corner to the upper right corner to make a diagonal fold. Unfold. Bring the lower right corner to the upper left corner to make the opposite fold. (Blue indicates right side, red the reverse side.)

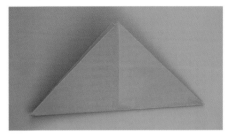

2. Unfold and turn the square over. Fold the square in half horizontally, matching the corners. Unfold. Fold the square in half vertically, matching the corners.

3. Unfold. With the right side facing up, refold the diagonal folds and push the horizontal folds inward to make a tree shape.

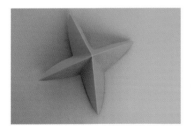

4. Fold over each outer edge toward the inner fold, creasing it with your thumbnail from the center top downward.

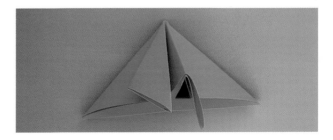

5. Four flaps now project downward. Fold each flap under along the lower edge of the tree.

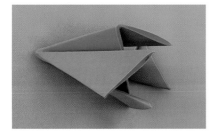 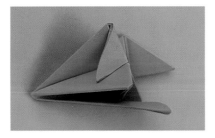

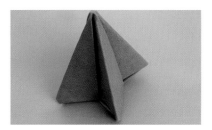

The finished tree stands alone.

6. Open the flaps of the tree partway, and glue or tape each flap tip tucked under the next. This makes a base for the tree.

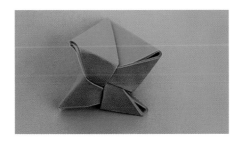

7. Sew a bead on the thread to use as a knot. Push the needle up through the tip inside the tree. Sew on a metal star or a string of beads, and tie a hook on the thread.

VARIATIONS

For a trimmed tree, glue on sequins, beads, and other accessories. Starting at the top, wrap a spiral of gold cord around the tree, gluing at each corner. Spiral the gold cord back up the tree, gluing at each corner, and glue it back to the top. Repeat steps #6 and #7 above to finish.

For a decorative tree, fold one square as above (steps #1 to #5), and hand punch holes randomly through the folded tree and along the diagonal edges (shown right). Unfold and align the metallic paper on the back of the first square. Glue both together, refold the tree, and glue or tape the flaps on the base.

25 *Fiber Christmas Tree*

Fill a clear Mylar (sheet vinyl) "sandwich" with yarns, floss, sequins, and stars to make a transparent Christmas tree ornament.

YOU NEED

- 12" x 15" clear Mylar*
- 3 hanks of embroidery floss in shades of green
- 4 gold 1¼" metal stars
- 24" gold cord
- Metallic trim, sequins, beads, or other flat embellishments
- 15" x ¾" ribbon
- Sewing machine, scissors, hand-sewing needle

Mylar® is a registered trademark of Dupont Teijin Films.

1. Trace the tree pattern on plain paper, or make two photocopies. These will serve not only as patterns, but they will also help the Mylar slide through the sewing machine.

2. Cut the Mylar into two 6" x 7½" sheets. Place one sheet of Mylar over a tree pattern. Clip the embroidery floss into 1" pieces. Sprinkle floss and stars, sequins, beads, or other trim on the pattern, overlapping the outline. Be sure no metal piece overlaps the seam line, or the sewing machine needle will break.

3. After you arrange the floss and decorations to suit you, cover them with the second Mylar sheet.

4. Place the second pattern on top of the "sandwich," aligned with the first pattern. Pin the pattern in place in the margins, and check for obstructions on the seam line.

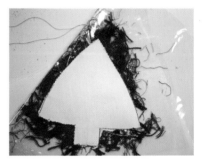

5. Using a long stitch (3.5 mm), sew along the pattern line. Hand-wheel over anything that might break the needle.

6. Remove the patterns. For easier removal, first score the stitch line with your thumbnail or a knitting needle, and then carefully tear away the stitch-perforated paper.

7. Cut around the tree, ¼" outside the stitch line through all the layers. Trim off any straggles.

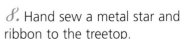

8. Hand sew a metal star and ribbon to the treetop.

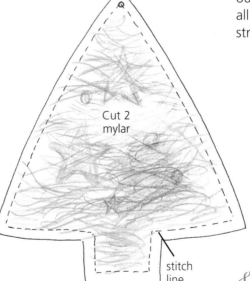

Cut 2 mylar

stitch line

TREE PATTERN
Photocopy at 200%.